A BEGINNERS GUIDE TO DECENTRALIZED FINANCE

Everything You Need To Know
About The DeFi

Reuben Ademola

Table of Contents

A BEGINNERS GUIDE TO DECENTRALIZED FINANCE

What is DeFi?

How can I earn interest on my cryptocurrency holdings with it?

What are the risks involved?

What impact does it have on the future of finance?

If you have these questions at the back of your mind, follow closely the information in this guide to handle these concerns and several others you may have.

Let us begin with the things you know:

-   A form of money that is not regulated by a central bank or government   are cryptocurrencies, an example is the bitcoin.

- Bitcoin is transferred from people around the world without the involvement of a bank or financial institution.

- Essentially, bitcoin is a decentralized money.

One of the common building blocks in a financial system is basically money exchange. There are other services that are in use today that centers around exchange that goes beyond sending money from one person to another. Loans, insurance, stock, saving plans are part of the services that create our financial system.

Presently, we run a centralized financial system and services. The organizational structure of banks, stock markets, insurance and several other financial institutions is vertical in nature with a financial executive or a board calling the shots and subordinates following orders.

The downside of a centralized financial system is numerous; some of the risks are mismanagement, fraud and corruption. So, what happens if the financial system is decentralized like the Bitcoin? That is where DeFi comes into the fray.

A financial system or service where there is no central authority is known as DeFi. With a decentralized medium of exchanging value like some cryptocurrencies, that can accept automated activities, exchanges, lending services, insurance organizations that does not rely on the arbiter of an individual or a board of executives will grow and nurture.

To create a decentralized financial system, infrastructure is a basic requirement to program and activate the decentralized services. The Ethereum blockchain is a network that fulfills this basic requisite.

DEFI COMPONENTS

1. Decentralized Infrastructure – Ethereum

The Ethereum network is a DIY platform for parsing decentralized programs that are called decentralized apps or Dapps. We write automated code which are referred to as smart contracts using Ethereum network. Smart contracts manage our financial services in a decentralized way.

We learn to assign the operational principles of a service that become automated when deployed on the Ethereum network. Once they are deployed, they become immutable and can no longer be changed.

When a system of this nature is available on a decentralized network, like that of Ethereum, the decentralized apps can then be used to create a decentralized financial system.

Let us examine the principles behind the whole thing:

2. Decentralized money – DIA

Money is required to fuel any financial system. And for a decentralized currency, we are not using bitcoin but Ether. Bitcoin is of course decentralized, and powered with a programmable functionality that is not compatible with the Ethereum network. Although, Ether is very volatile, it is compatible and programmable.

To build reliable financial services that people will continue to use, currency stability is necessary to work the system. It is the point where we can talk about stablecoins.

The value of stablecoins is attached to the value of real world assets, for example the US dollar. Because we want to eliminate the central control of value where a stablecoin is pegged to reserve money in fiat, another concept known as DIA is introduced.

DIA is basically decentralized cryptocurrency that is pegged against the value of the US dollar, consequently, one DIA is the same as one US dollar. While several stablecoins are pegged to US dollar reserves, DIA uses crypto collaterals which is displayed as a public ledger on the Ethereum blockchain.

If you put in a deposit of $1 of Ether, you can access 66 cents DIA as loan. For DIA, the concept is called over collateral. When you want to get your Ether value back, pay off the DIA loan to get your Ether, purchase DIA as an exchange when there is no Ether locked up as collateral.

While the price of Ether may be volatile, or at worse, extremely volatile, the value of the Ether backing the DIA that has been locked remains secure, or perhaps increase.

Therefore, the DIA stablecoin is a smart contract that exists on the Ethereum platform, which powers the trustless and decentralized stablecoin that cannot be censored; a perfect type of money as exchange for DeFi services.

3. DEX

Since our decentralized financial system has a decentralized money that is stable, we can now implant several services on the platform. Let us examine the first use case called the decentralized exchange or simply the DEX.

Depending on the operating principles and smart contracts, DEX encourage users to buy, sell, or trade cryptocurrencies. Because they are more like DIA, they are decentralized.

Some of the things that you don't deal with when exchanging a DEX are exchange operators, sign-ups, identity verification, and withdrawal fees. The smart contracts enforce all transaction rules, handles the trade, and handle your funds securely. If it were a centralized financial exchange, you may have to deposit funds into an exchange account before a trade happens. A decentralized platform removes the risk of hacking an exchange of asset or information, a common problem for all centralized exchanges.

- Money market

The possibilities of decentralized financial services are limitless. Let us quickly evaluate a decentralized money market, one that connect borrowers with lenders as a service. With Compound, an Ethereum lending and borrowing dapp, lend and earn interest on your crypto with ease and even earn interest. Also, pay your rent or buy groceries with cryptocurrencies too. If this one appeals to you, deposit your crypto as collateral and borrow against it.

The Compound platform brings lenders and borrowers together, and deploys the operational principles automatically for the loans and the manner the interest earned are distributed. Lately, there has been a remarkable popularity with earning interest on cryptocurrencies, a trend that has birthed "yield farming".

Yield farming simply means allowing your crypto assets work while attempting to drain the optimal returns from it as much as possible.

- Insurance

Presently, we have decentralized stablecoins, decentralized exchanges and fully decentralized money markets. These financial products are not risk-averse; therefore, for some people, they want to know why their funds cannot be insured when the system suffers a loss?

For a decentralized insurance organization, one that brings people that are paying for insurance and connects them to those that are running a premium insurance without the need for an intermediary, agent or broker, is definitely good news.

Besides, DeFi services run with several others seamlessly where several services can be interchanged to create new and exciting opportunities. It is how you use LEGO blocks and become creative with what you are creating. The term "money legos" is now a metaphorical expression for DeFi services. The following services are built using several money legos:

- First, you need a decentralized aggregator to know the best exchange rate for Ether and DAI

- Choose the DEX of your choice and complete the exchange.

- Earn an interest on the loaned out DIA to lenders.

- Include insurance to the process for financial safety reasons.

There are several opportunities for DeFi, the one illustrated above is just an example. You can begin to imagine the advantages of DeFi; some of them are:

- Transparency

- Interoperability

- Decentralization

- Open to all services.

- User experience is flexible.

Apart from the merits of the system, there are also some risks:

- DeFi is a new concept, and with all new things, there is a chance of things going wrong. In the past, smart contracts did not define the operational principles of certain services allowing hackers to exploit the loopholes to steal money.

- If you are testing a DeFi service, start with a disposable amount that you won't lose sleep over in the event that it fails.

- A system is decentralized at its core which means that services appear to be decentralized but hold traces of centralization which could lead to the failure of the system.

- Know the rudiments of a product or service before you invest. Learning about a product or service let you know its risks

The DeFi revolution is best described as a new concept that is gradually finding space at an early adopter level.

Its complete adoption depends on how people accepts it.

But a decentralized financial system will bring a lot of benefit to the population, especially those going through the risks akin to traditional financial systems such as inefficiencies and high fees.

WHAT IS DEFI?

Running along with traditional financial tools and transferring them to a blockchain is what a decentralized financial service is all about.

A few of the services running on the decentralized financial services are loans, trade, and savings. There are about $2 billion of cryptocurrency asset kept inside the DeFi protocols, a trend that has quad-tripled the last year.

Several DeFi projects are created on the Ethereum blockchain as Ethereum is leading other cryptocurrencies in decentralized finance.

One, smart contracts are supported on Ethereum which are programs that are created on the blockchain.

Besides, after bitcoin, Ethereum is the second market capitalization cryptocurrency. Ethereum is a popular blockchain and it is the platform for moving into DeFi and other apps that are supported by Ethereum.

That they take much resemblance to a regular website means nothing as they actually use smart contracts to interact with the blockchain.

WHY DEFI?

Partaking in decentralized finance comes with its own benefits unlike traditional system such as:

- Competitive interest rates

- Yield farming

- Eth token – purchasing market cap cryptocurrencies in fractions that are not listed on the popular exchanges.

There are several reasons to partake in DeFi as its use cases are being realized with the expansion of the space. Few of the benefits for casual users are listed after you understand its requisites:

1. Holding a minimum Ethereum cryptocurrency to use as gas fees. Gas fees are paid with ether to facilitate a transaction.

One of the convenient ways to get some ether is a website like coinbase.com or Binance. Purchase Cryptocurrency with your bank account or debit card. Releasing your bank account information or debit card, which are entered into KYC is an inherent risk that you are taking. Create a Coinbase account to get started. It is a multi-step process for identifying and verifying your account or ID. Remember that sign up and the time you can start purchasing cryptocurrency is different. Once you have set up the payment gateway, include a payment method using a bank account or debit card. Debit for several people is usually the safest and easiest, for a small gwei. Tap prices and find Ethereum, only 15 dollars.

Because you are paying gas fees on the apps, register with more than 5 dollars. Only part with what you can lose that will not cost you sleep. $15 is a great starting point. Tap on preview buy and check how the fees are itemized before going ahead with clicking Buy now. It takes some time before the funds become available to you.

You can start trading your ether immediately although you may have to wait three days to withdraw it.

2. First, connect an Ethereum wallet to your browser.

Since a lot of people use chrome, use Metamask with google chrome because Metamask is quite easy to install. Visit the Google chrome store to search for Metamask, and then tap install.

First, you need a special browser extension to use a dapp or other DeFi applications. Another thing is that several browsers don't accept connection to the blockchain unlike Metamask.

Another requirement is having a cryptocurrency in your wallet. Metamask also works as a wallet allowing you to manage your account and sign the transaction to use the DeFi apps.

When Metamask has been installed, set up your wallet. The setup process takes you through a few steps that involves the recovery phrase that you must back up and share with no other person. After this, set up a password to protect your Metamask account.

When everything is set up, you will have an account that runs on the Ethereum network. Your username or email address is used to identify you on the Ethereum network. You also have a private key attached to it as well, something similar to a password.

Withdraw some cryptocurrency from Coinbase and transfer it into your Metamask wallet. Click send once you are done.

The buy button becomes gray until after three days. Tap send and paste in your address that you copied from metamask. You will receive an email confirmation once it is deposited into your wallet. When everything is wrapped up, you should regularly check your balance there.

Check your transaction log with ether scan where your deposit history will be displayed. Now that your DeFi apps are ready to be used, let us try the decentralized exchange.

Tap your URL bar and input one-inch dot exchange. Operating like a Coinbase, it is a decentralized exchange that is powered by the blockchain.

WHAT DOES A DECENTRALIZED EXCHANGE (DEX) DO?

Buy and sell tokens at a fixed price. Rather than opening a limit order on a cryptocurrency exchange and watch as the charge that looks like a candlestick run out, you are only given its price and swap it immediately. It is similar to using the Coinbase purchase feature from your bank account. If you have a cryptocurrency, you can purchase another one. You must hold cryptocurrency to use the app since it runs on a blockchain. An inch is basically a DEX aggregator and requires several decentralized exchanges to give you the best price after combining everything in a place.

Why use a DEX?

The benefits of using DEX as opposed to Coinbase or Binance are listed below:

- Non-custodial: your money is not controlled by the app unlike Coinbase. If you trade with cryptocurrencies on your exchange, having a level of trust is necessary to continue exchanging large or small cryptocurrencies.

- No KYC: giving them your ID documents before using the application is not necessary. Besides, having a minimum deposit is also not required.

- Small tokens: there is an opportunity to purchase smaller market cap tokens unlisted on the major exchange. Several of these tokens are increasing in the Ethereum blockchain, purchase them on one-inch exchange if you cannot find them on Coinbase.

- Instant Swap: there are instant swap features that are commonplace when dealing with DEXes.

Now let us quickly talk about how to swap ether for DAI

DAI is an immutable cryptocurrency like a stablecoin. It is part of the DeFi ecosystem where dollar is stable against changes in prices. Use a small amount of ether from your wallet and purchase some DAI, once you are done, click swap.

From there, you will learn to use Metamask. There is also the gas fee that is available which is costly. Prepare to spend $15 worth of Ethereum to purchase the DIA's gas fee rather than the real DAI itself.

Tap on Verify and soon a Metamask confirmation is displayed.

Edit the gas fee too, for instance if you wish to take more time, slow down its pace.

Tap save and wait to see that your transaction has been sent.

The transaction receipt is open on etherscan which displays all the details.

Since you have purchased the DAI, add it to the wallet. Click DAI to go through the smart contract page on etherscan.

Copy the smart contract address and enter Metamask to "Add token". Once you do that, click "Custom token". Paste the smart contract and tap Next.

Eventually, your DAI balance becomes available. There is also a list of your tokens on a column and DAI at the bottom. Once you have secured a few DAI, let us use another application.

On your browser, input compound finance into the URL bar. Compound is a savings and lending app that runs on a blockchain. It is a DeFi app that utilizes smart contracts.

How does it work? Tap on the app and discover two ways to use the app, either by supplying or borrowing.

The idea behind the whole thing is earning interest on a cryptocurrency. Of course, you will deal with competitive interest rates which will vary; some as high as 8-10% before going down.

This concept is particularly interesting for everyday users of blockchain technology since you may purchase a cryptocurrency like DAI whose price is immutable and transfer it to Compound where you earn a competitive interest rate which is far better than what saving in your traditional bank will give you. The ability to earn such interest is as a result of borrowing cryptocurrency through a collateralized loan.

HOW TO MOVE CRYPTOCURRENCY TO COMPOUND?

You will see a confirmation pop up for Metamask the first time that you use the Dapp. It simply requests that you connect to Compound. Confirm the request so that you don't see the prompt anymore. Because we are only supplying a few DAI, tap on DAI and select "supply". You will be asked to enable it.

A Metamask confirmation pop up will be displayed that you can tap to confirm. Once you select max, you will see all the DAI that you have. Select "supply" for a Metamask confirmation pop up.

The gas fee to pay is high. If you don't have enough money for it, edit and click on slow, and then save. The time for all this will not exceed 10 minutes to make confirmation.

Once you are through, view the transaction on etherscan. A small screen shows you the transaction details where the DAI has changed to C DAI, also showing your APY (annual percentage yield), current balance, and your balance gradually increasing once you begin to earn interest. It is how compound works and how you mix it up with an app like Metamask and others.

Compound is a substitute for your bank where you begin to earn interest rates and allow people borrow funds using collateralized loans.

Mobile Ethereum wallet

There is also the mobile Ethereum wallet that we will briefly demonstrate its use. We will use Trust Wallet. This wallet is used to keep tabs on your assets or trade cryptocurrencies once prices change. It is particularly good for short-term trading.

With your Metamask wallet, go to Settings. Click Wallet and tap "Create a new wallet". Tap "I have a wallet already". You will receive a prompt that ask you to input your Metamask recovery phrase. Click on "export wallet" on your Metamask app to find your recovery phrase. Export the private key one by one. Once you are done, click import. The cryptocurrency that you have in your Metamask wallet shows up automatically when it is imported.

Other things that you can do with the wallet apart from trading are the following:

- Enable face ID recognition on your iPhone to disallow others from gaining access to your account or funds.

- Transfer cryptocurrency tokens to anyone directly from your wallet.

- Scan your QR codes.

- Swap tokens from the app. If you are purchasing these small market cap cryptocurrencies from the app that are not fully supported on major exchanges.

- Deploy on-ramp and off-ramp protocols with your wallet.

Five methods to invest in DeFi in 2021

1. Invest within DeFi: there are several applications and protocols that perform different actions. RV and Compound are platforms that gives you a better interest rate, and could pay as well as lend crypto to other people. Almost similar to the traditional financial system, where you earn from lending money to others. DeFi, an open and decentralized platform, allows you to realize your financial potential. Also, make money as a liquidity provider. How to do this? Set some funds aside on a decentralized exchange like uniswap, where you provide liquidity to users on the platform. Also, you can earn governance tokens released by the protocols for borrowing and lending out cryptocurrencies as a yield

farmer to earn the largest yields.

These are a few means of earning from DeFi. Know that there are some risks involved with the process that you must be cognizant of going forward. Not minding these things lead to losing your money.

There are two huge risks when using these protocols:

- You will deal with smart contracts, bugs or exploits. The money that flows in the DeFi ecosystem is transmitted through or stored in smart contracts. Because of the nature of asset storage, smart contracts are often liable to exploitation as mistakes may arise from the intentional or accidental exploitation of the contract or the code, which leads to the assets in the smart contract lost forever.

- Another cause is bad actors: on a decentralized exchange like uniswap, which is also basically a permission less system, anyone can add tokens to generate hype and interest on social media. Even those with bad intention can invest so much ether in the liquidity pool, unknown to them, there is a back door within the code which permits those that created the token to take the all Ethereum assets. In DeFi parlance, it is called "getting rug pulled". It is another risk that you need to be aware of to remain in the system.

2. Investing or Speculating on the DeFi tokens: Several DeFi apps

have tokens that you can sell or buy. First, purchase a token when it is low and sell it once it gains traction. Although it really sounds simple, it is not like that in reality. Quality is not an important consideration if you are planning to speculate or trade tokens of this nature. Just be mindful of the price. Be aware that of speculating risks regardless of the platform being decentralized. The fact is that you may earn a lot of money like its lottery and also lose a lot like a windfall. Do your due diligence as a speculator, to pick the gem from the garbage as there are a lot of garbage out there that are disguised as gems. Evaluate the tokens to determine their quality and optimize your chances of selecting projects that are sustainable in the long term. If you are investing or wish to speculate on tokens, there are several ways to do that. In fact, there are several coins that you can start investing in from a decentralized exchange platform. An example is uniswap, others you can get on the standard centralized exchanges like Binance. There is a default section for the exchangers where you can pick the tokens to invest. Nowadays, you can look for them on several fiat exchanges like Coinbase. You can access the DeFi tokens to invest or speculate on several platforms.

3. Getting exposure to a DeFi index: if you have invested in index funds some times before,

you know that such investment opens you to the stock market where you can benchmark prices of the stock market rather than selectin individual organizations that may not perform better on the average of the whole index. The same approach can be replicated for decentralized finance too. If you wish to spread your risk, and not bet all you have on a single project, pick your fund exposure to a selected number of coins. On the other hand, you may simply have exposure to your DeFi index.

4. Betting or exposing your investment to the underlying protocol that the DeFi ecosystem is implanted upon: DeFi contains several applications of smart contracts

that is powered by an underlying protocol, on a blockchain network that is spearheaded by Ethereum. As an ecosystem, it works on Ethereum unlike smaller blockchain networks where this operation is non-existent. An example of a smaller blockchain network is Polkadot. Perhaps you are bullish on DeFi as a trend or technological movement, and you are carefully trying to avoid exposing your investments to any project out there; even an exposure to a DeFi index is not on your roadmap, it is alright. Be involved in a simple bet to invest in the underlying protocol where the buzzing activity is in progress. To invest in the underlying protocol is very straightforward just like

DeFi on Ethereum where people want to latch on the trend of using DeFi on Ethereum which requires paying the necessary gas fees to use the protocol. Besides, they also purchase ether for other reasons such as staking, trading or purchasing ERC 20 tokens. If the demand for buying Ethereum is on the rise, it is an indication that the market is bullish as people want to use the DeFi ecosystem. Such indication will guide you to set individual price. For a cautious investor, the safest approach to investing in the DeFi ecosystem is to check for bullish indicators before setting a price. You don't have to be concerned about individual exposure to your individual projects as the non-performance of a coin does not even affect the integrity of your underlying protocol as a whole. And the fact is that Ethereum will survive even though DeFi projects die off.

5. Bet on projects that depend on the DeFi ecosystem to sustain the growth of the DeFi.: you need to get your creative juices flowing to think holistically of the DeFi ecosystem as a space that will continue to expand and grow over the years. If it eventually explodes in growth, think about the projects that will directly benefit from such growth in the future. What type of demand is existing for these projects in response to DeFi activities presently? Once DeFi grows in the long term, what are the related services that

will be talked about or remain relevant? One example of a sustainable potential opportunity is Oracle. Several DeFi applications will use oracles to get the right data price and other relevant market information that the applications will depend on to work properly. In fact, a greater demand for DeFi is commensurate with a greater demand for oracle. In theory, we can also assume that a greater demand for oracle is equal to the bullish price attached to oracle tokens. Invest in oracle coins out there as you wish. You can as well create an exposure to chain link, which is a spot that demands your creativity as there are several opportunities that you can tap into when

DeFi finally explodes in size and demand. It is just a matter of thinking about the opportunities the market will demand going forward. The five ways listed above are the means to inest in DeFi in 2021. If there is any takeaway from this conversation, it is that there is no one-size-fits-all approach. Evaluate your personal requirements, risk profile, time horizon, competency level, expertise and go with what tickles your fancy most. Think along the lines of what inspires you to perform qualitative research to choose right. Now, that is what no one will do for you but yourself.